"Caring for kids with down syndrome in the Class'

A Practical guide for Educators

By Uzuegbu Joy

CHAPTER ONE

INTRODUCTION

A. Overview of Down syndrome

Down syndrome, also known as Trisomy 21, is a genetic disorder caused by the presence of an extra copy of chromosome 21. This extra genetic material leads to the characteristic physical and cognitive features of the disorder.

Physical characteristics of Down syndrome can include a flat facial profile, small head and ears, upward slanting eyes, and a short neck. Individuals with Down syndrome may also have joint and muscle weakness, which can lead to delays in motor development and difficulty with fine motor skills.

Cognitively, individuals with Down syndrome may have intellectual disabilities, with an average IQ of around 50-70. They may also have difficulty with memory and processing information, as well as learning new tasks. However, with early intervention and appropriate support, many individuals with Down syndrome can learn new skills and achieve their full potential.

Down syndrome is a lifelong condition and it can also lead to other health problems such as respiratory and ear infections, heart defects, and problems with vision and hearing.

However, with proper medical care and support, many individuals with Down syndrome can live healthy and fulfilling lives.

It is usually diagnosed at birth by a physical examination and confirmed by a chromosomal analysis. It occurs in 1 in 700 live births, and it is the most common chromosomal disorder.

It is not caused by anything the parents did or did not do, and the risk of having a child with Down syndrome increases as the mother gets older. There is no cure for Down syndrome, but early intervention, special education, and therapy can help improve the development of children with Down syndrome and improve their quality of life.

B. The Importance of Education for Children with Down syndrome

Education plays a vital role in the development and well-being of children with Down syndrome. It provides them with the opportunity to acquire the skills and knowledge necessary to lead fulfilling and independent lives.

Here are some of the reasons why education is important for children with Down syndrome:

Cognitive Development: Education provides children with Down syndrome with the opportunity to develop their cognitive abilities and improve their intellectual functioning. This can include learning basic skills such as reading, writing, and math, as well as more complex skills such as problem-solving and critical thinking.

Language and Communication: Children with Down syndrome often have delays in language and communication development. Education can help them to improve their language and communication skills, which are essential for effective communication and social interactions.

Socialization: Education provides children with Down syndrome with the opportunity to interact with their peers and develop social skills. This can include learning how to make friends, share, take turns, and follow rules.

Independence: Education can help children with Down syndrome to develop the skills and knowledge necessary to lead independent lives. This can include learning self-care skills, such as dressing and grooming, as well as practical skills such as cooking and budgeting.

Confidence and Self-Esteem: Education can help children with Down syndrome to develop confidence and self-esteem. This can include learning new skills and achieving academic milestones, as well as being recognized for their unique strengths and abilities.

In conclusion, education is crucial for the development and well-being of children with Down syndrome. It provides them with the opportunity to acquire the skills and knowledge necessary to lead fulfilling and independent lives and helps them to develop cognitively, socially and emotionally. With the right support and accommodations, children with Down syndrome can succeed in school and reach their full potential

C. Importance of inclusion in mainstream classrooms

Inclusion in mainstream classrooms is important for children with Down syndrome because it provides them with opportunities to learn and grow alongside their typically developing peers.

Here are a few key benefits of inclusion:

Increased socialization and peer interactions: Being in a mainstream classroom allows children with Down syndrome to interact with and learn from typically developing peers, which can help improve their social skills and self-esteem.

Access to age-appropriate curriculum: Inclusion in mainstream classrooms ensures that children with Down

Syndrome have access to age-appropriate curriculum and instruction, which can help them reach their full potential.

Development of independence and self-advocacy skills: Inclusion in mainstream classrooms allows children with Down syndrome to learn and practice important life skills, such as self-care, problem-solving, and self-advocacy, which will be useful for them in the future.

Improved academic achievement: Children with Down syndrome who are included in mainstream classrooms have been shown to have better academic outcomes than those in segregated settings.

Positive impact on typically developing peers: Inclusive classrooms have been shown to have a positive impact on typically developing peers, as they learn to appreciate and value diversity, and can also learn valuable life skills, such as patience, kindness, and empathy.

It's important to note that inclusion in a mainstream classroom can be challenging, and that it might require additional support and accommodations for the child with Down Syndrome. But with proper planning, training, and support, it can be a very positive and beneficial experience for the child and the entire class.

CHAPTER TWO

MANAGING A DOWN SYNDROME CHILD IN THE CLASSROOM

Managing a child with Down syndrome in the classroom can present unique challenges for educators. However, with the right support and accommodations, it is possible to create an inclusive and supportive environment where the child can thrive.

Here are some strategies for managing a Down syndrome child in the classroom:

Creating an Inclusive and Supportive Environment: It is important to create a classroom environment that is inclusive and welcoming for children with Down syndrome. This can include providing visual aids, such as pictures and diagrams, to help with understanding, as well as using positive reinforcement and rewards to encourage good behavior.

Adapting Curriculum and Materials: Children with Down syndrome may have delays in their cognitive and language development. Educators should adapt the curriculum and materials to meet the child's needs. This can include using multisensory teaching methods, such as incorporating visual and hands-on activities, to help the child understand and retain information.

Strategies for Managing Behavior: Children with Down syndrome may have difficulty with self-regulation and may display challenging behaviors. Educators should use positive behavior management strategies, such as providing clear rules and consequences, and using visual schedules and social stories to help the child understand expectations.

Collaboration with Parents and Caregivers: Collaboration between educators and parents/caregivers is essential for the success of a child with Down syndrome in the classroom. Educators should communicate regularly with the parents/caregivers to share information about the child's progress and any concerns that may arise.

Differentiated instruction: Children with Down syndrome have different learning styles, strengths and weaknesses. It is important to differentiate instruction and provide individualized support to meet the child's needs. This can include providing extra support in certain subjects or using technology to support learning.

In conclusion, managing a child with Down syndrome in the classroom requires a comprehensive approach that includes creating an inclusive and supportive environment, adapting curriculum and materials, using positive behavior management strategies, and collaborating with parents and caregivers. With the right support and accommodations, children with Down syndrome can succeed in the classroom and reach their full potential.

A. Creating an Inclusive and Supportive Environment for a Down syndrome Child

Creating an inclusive and supportive environment in the classroom is essential for the success of a child with Down syndrome. Here are some strategies and examples of how to create such an environment:

1. **Use visual aids:** Children with Down syndrome may have difficulty processing and understanding verbal information Using visual aids, such as pictures, diagrams, and videos, can help to supplement verbal instruction and make learning more concrete. For example, a teacher can use a visual schedule to help a child understand the order of events for the day or use a social story to explain a new routine or rule.

2. **Provide extra support and accommodations**: Children with Down syndrome may need extra

support and accommodations to access the curriculum and participate in class activities. For example, a child may need extra time to complete assignments, or the teacher may need to use a communication device to help the child express themselves.

3. **Encourage peer interactions**: Children with Down syndrome may have difficulty interacting with their peers, so it's important to provide opportunities for them to interact and socialize with other students. For example, the teacher can create small group activities that encourage cooperation and communication among students.

4. **Use positive reinforcement:** Children with Down syndrome may need extra encouragement and positive reinforcement to build self-esteem and motivation. The teacher can use positive reinforcement strategies such as praising the child for good behavior, academic achievement, or effort.

5. **Create a safe and comfortable environment:** Children with Down syndrome may have sensory sensitivities, so it's important to create a safe and comfortable environment in the classroom. For example, the teacher can use calming colors on the walls and provide a quiet space for the child to relax when they need it.

In conclusion, creating an inclusive and supportive environment for a child with Down syndrome requires an understanding of the child's unique needs and the use of strategies and accommodations that are tailored to meet those needs. By using visual aids, providing extra support and accommodations, encouraging peer interactions, using positive reinforcement, and creating a safe and comfortable environment,

B. Adapting Curriculum and Materials

Children with Down syndrome may have delays in their cognitive and language development, so it's important to adapt the curriculum and materials to meet their needs. Here are some strategies and examples of how to adapt curriculum and materials for a child with Down syndrome:

1. **Use multisensory teaching methods:** Children with Down syndrome often benefit from multisensory teaching methods that incorporate visual, auditory, and hands-on activities. For example, a teacher can use manipulative, such as counting bears, to teach math concepts, or use a puppet to act out a story to help a child understand the plot.

2. **Provide extra support and repetition:** Children with Down syndrome may need extra support and repetition to understand and retain information. For example, a teacher can provide extra practice sheets for math or reading, or use flashcards to help a child learn new vocabulary words.

3. **Use technology**: Technology can be an effective tool for adapting curriculum and materials for a child with Down syndrome. For example, a teacher can use a text-to-speech program to help a child read, or use an app to help a child learn math facts.

4. **Use visual aids:** Using visual aids, such as pictures and diagrams, can help a child with Down syndrome to understand and retain information. For example, a teacher can use a visual schedule to help a child understand the order of events for the day, or use a flowchart to help a child understand the steps in a process.

5. **Differentiate instruction:** Children with Down syndrome have different learning styles, strengths, and weaknesses, so it's important to differentiate instruction to meet their individual needs. For example, a teacher can provide extra support in certain subjects or use technology to support learning.

C. Strategies for Managing Behavior

Children with Down syndrome may have difficulty with self-regulation and may display challenging behaviors. It's important for educators to use positive behavior management strategies to help manage these behaviors. Here are some strategies and examples of how to manage behavior for a child with Down syndrome:

1. **Use visual cues and schedules**: Children with Down syndrome may have difficulty understanding verbal instructions, so using visual cues and schedules can help them understand expectations and routines. For example, a teacher can use a visual schedule to help a child understand the order of events for the day, or use picture icons to remind a child of the rules.

2. **Use positive reinforcement:** Children with Down syndrome may need extra encouragement and positive reinforcement to build self-esteem and motivation. A teacher can use positive reinforcement strategies such as praising the child

for good behavior, academic achievement, or effort. For example, a teacher can give a child a sticker or a token for completing a task or following a rule.

3. **Teach self-regulation skills:** Children with Down syndrome may have difficulty regulating their emotions, so it's important to teach them self-regulation skills. For example, a teacher can teach a child to use deep breathing or other relaxation techniques when they feel upset or anxious.

4. **Use social stories:** Social stories can be an effective tool for teaching children with Down syndrome about social skills, routines, and expected behaviors. For example, a teacher can create a social story about how to take turns or how to wait patiently for a turn.

5. **Collaborate with parents and caregivers**: Collaboration between educators and parents/caregivers is essential for the success of a child with Down syndrome in the classroom.

Educators should communicate regularly with the parents/caregivers to share information about the child's progress and any concerns that may arise, and work together to develop a behavior plan that is tailored to the child's needs.

D. Collaboration with Parents and Caregivers

Collaboration with parents and caregivers is essential for effectively handling a child with Down syndrome: Collaboration between parents and caregivers can be incredibly beneficial for a child with Down syndrome. By working together, parents and caregivers can ensure that the child receives the most effective and comprehensive care possible.

Here are some ways that collaboration between parents and caregivers can help a child with Down syndrome:

1. **Sharing information:** Parents and caregivers can share important information about the child's development, behavior, and progress. This can help caregivers understand the child's unique needs and strengths, and adjust their approach accordingly. For example, a parent may know that the child has difficulty with fine motor skills, and the caregiver can incorporate activities that help with this.

2. **Developing a consistent approach:** Parents and caregivers can work together to develop a consistent approach to care and education. This can help the child feel more secure and reduce confusion. For example, if a parent is teaching the child how to count at home, the caregiver can continue this work in the classroom.

3. **Setting goals:** Parents and caregivers can set goals for the child's development and work together to achieve them. For example, if the goal is to improve the child's speech, the parent can work on speech exercises at home, and the caregiver can work on speech therapy in the classroom.

4. **Monitoring progress:** Parents and caregivers can work together to monitor the child's progress and make adjustments as needed. For example, if the child is not making progress in a certain area, the parent and caregiver can work together to develop a new approach.

5. **Creating a support network**: Collaboration between parents and caregivers can help create a support network for the child. The child can see that their parents and caregivers are working together to help them, which can give them a sense of security and belonging.

6. **Building open communication:** Collaboration between parents and caregivers can also help establish open and honest communication. This can help ensure that any concerns or issues are addressed quickly and effectively. For example, if the caregiver notices that the child is struggling with a particular task, they can inform the parent and work together to find a solution.

7. **Communication**: Keeping open lines of communication is crucial for ensuring that the child's needs are being met. Parents and caregivers should discuss the child's development, behavior, and any concerns they may have, and work together to create a plan of action.

8. **Education:** Parents and caregivers should educate themselves about Down syndrome, including the child's physical and intellectual capabilities, as well as the best methods for supporting their development. This can include learning about therapy and special education programs, as well as researching the latest research and resources available.

9. **Support:** Parents and caregivers should work together to provide emotional and practical support

for the child and each other. This can include taking turns watching the child, sharing responsibilities, and providing emotional support during difficult times.

10. **Advocacy**: Parents and caregivers should advocate for the child's needs and rights, including working with schools, healthcare providers, and other organizations to ensure that the child has access to the resources and services they need.

11. **Encouragement:** Parents and caregivers should encourage the child to be independent and reach their full potential. This can include providing opportunities for the child to learn new skills, participate in activities, and make their own choices

It's important to note that every child with Down syndrome is unique and will have their own specific needs and strengths. Collaboration between parents and caregivers can help ensure that the child receives the best possible care, tailored to their individual needs

CHAPTER THREE

TEACHING A DOWN SYNDROME CHILD

Teaching a child with Down Syndrome can be a unique and rewarding experience. It is important to understand that each child with Down Syndrome is an individual and may have different strengths and weaknesses. However, there are some general strategies that can be used to help these children learn effectively.

One key strategy is to use a multi-sensory approach to teaching. This means using a variety of different methods to present information, such as visual aids, hands-on activities, and verbal explanations. For example, when teaching a child with Down Syndrome about the alphabet, you could use flashcards with pictures to represent each letter, have the child trace the letters with their finger, and also say the name of the letter out loud.

Another important strategy is to break down tasks and instructions into small, manageable steps. Children with Down Syndrome often have difficulty with complex tasks and may become overwhelmed if given too much information at once. For example, instead of asking a child with Down Syndrome to write a whole sentence, you could start by having them trace over the letters of the alphabet, then work on forming simple words, and gradually build up to writing complete sentences.

It is also important to use positive reinforcement and to be patient when working with a child with Down Syndrome. These children may take longer to understand and complete tasks, and may need extra encouragement and praise to stay motivated.

It is crucial to work with the child's strengths and interests. Children with Down Syndrome often have strong visual and auditory memory. Therefore, it could be beneficial to use songs, rhymes, and visual aids to teach new concepts.

In addition, it is important to provide opportunities for the child with Down Syndrome to practice and apply new skills in real-life situations. For example, if the child is learning how to count, you could have them practice counting objects around the house, such as the number of shoes in the closet or the number of cookies on a plate.

Finally, it is essential to work closely with the child's parents and other professionals, such as speech therapists, occupational therapists, and special education teachers, to develop an individualized education plan that meets the child's unique needs.

In summary, teaching a child with Down syndrome requires a multi-sensory approach, breaking down tasks and instructions into small manageable steps, positive reinforcement, patience, working with child's strengths and interests, providing opportunities for practice and application of new skills, and close collaboration with parents and other professionals

A. Developmental Milestones and Learning Styles

Down Syndrome (DS) is a genetic disorder caused by an extra copy of chromosome 21. Children with Down Syndrome experience delays in physical, cognitive, and language development. These delays can affect the child's ability to learn and can impact their developmental milestones.

Physical Development:

Children with Down Syndrome typically have delays in their physical development. They may take longer to learn to sit, crawl, walk and run. They may also have low muscle tone, which can make it harder for them to control their movements and maintain balance. They may also have difficulty with fine motor skills, such as grasping small objects and using utensils.

Cognitive Development:

Cognitive development can also be affected by Down Syndrome. Children with DS may have difficulty with problem-solving, memory, and attention.

They may also have difficulty with abstract concepts, such as time and money. They often have difficulty with learning new information and may require more repetition and practice to grasp a new concept.

Language Development:

Children with Down Syndrome may have difficulty with language development. They may have delayed speech and language development, difficulty with articulation, and difficulty understanding and using language. They may also have difficulty with social communication skills, such as taking turns in conversation and understanding nonverbal cues.

Learning Styles:

Every child is unique, and children with Down syndrome have their specific learning styles. However, some general characteristics that may influence the learning of a child with Down Syndrome are:

i.   They tend to have strong visual memory, so using visual aids such as flashcards, pictures and videos can be helpful.

ii.   They may have difficulty with abstract concepts and may require more concrete examples and hands-on activities to understand new information.

iii. They may have difficulty with attention and memory, so breaking down tasks into smaller steps and providing frequent reminders may be necessary.

iv.   They may have difficulty with fine motor skills, so using manipulative and hands-on activities can be helpful.

v.   They may have difficulty with language, so using gestures, pictures, and other forms of nonverbal communication can be beneficial.

vi.   They may have difficulty with social communication skills, so providing opportunities for social interactions and practicing social skills in a supportive environment can be helpful.

In summary, Children with Down Syndrome may experience delays in their physical, cognitive, and language development.

They often have difficulty with problem-solving, memory, attention, and abstract concepts, and may require more repetition and practice to grasp new information. They tend to have strong visual memory, and may benefit from visual aids, hands-on activities, and breaking down tasks into smaller steps. Additionally, providing opportunities for social interactions and practicing social skills in a supportive environment can also be beneficial

B. Strategies for Teaching Language and Communication

Teaching language and communication to a child with Down syndrome can be challenging, as these children often have delayed speech and language development. However, there are several strategies that can be used to help these children learn to communicate effectively.

i. **Use a multi-modal approach:** Children with Down Syndrome often have strong visual memory and may benefit from visual aids such as flashcards, pictures, and videos to help them understand new words and concepts. Using a combination of verbal explanations, gestures, and nonverbal communication can also be helpful.

ii. **Break down language into smaller parts:** Children with Down Syndrome may have difficulty understanding complex language, so breaking down language into smaller, more manageable parts can be helpful. For example, instead of teaching a child a whole sentence, you could start by teaching them individual words and then gradually building up to complete sentences.

iii. **Use repetition and practice:** Children with Down Syndrome often require more repetition and practice to grasp new concepts.

It is important to provide opportunities for the child to practice their language skills in a variety of different settings and with different people.

iv. **Use social stories**: Social stories are short, simple stories that describe a situation or a social skill in a clear and concrete way. They can be used to teach children with Down Syndrome about different social situations and how to respond appropriately.

v. **Encourage the child to communicate:** Children with Down Syndrome may have difficulty initiating communication, so it is important to provide opportunities for them to communicate and to encourage them to do so. For example, you could ask open-ended questions, give them choices, and provide positive feedback when they initiate communication.

vi. **Use sign language:** Sign language can be a useful tool for teaching children with Down Syndrome who have difficulty with speech and language. It can be used to teach new words and concepts and to provide a means of communication before the child is able to speak.

vii. **Collaborate with other professionals:** Children with Down syndrome often require support from a variety of different professionals, such as speech therapists, occupational therapists, and special education teachers. It is important to work closely with these professionals to develop an individualized education plan that meets the child's unique needs.

In summary, teaching language and communication to a child with Down Syndrome requires a multi-modal approach, breaking down language into smaller parts, repetition, and practice, using social stories, encouraging the child to communicate, using sign language, and collaborating with other professionals. These strategies may help the child to acquire language and communication skills, and improve their ability to express themselves and interact with others.

C. Strategies for Teaching Math and Reading

Teaching math and reading to a child with Down syndrome can present some unique challenges, but there are several strategies that can be used to help make the learning process more effective.

i. **Use visual aids:** Children with Down syndrome often have difficulty processing verbal information, so visual aids such as pictures, diagrams, and manipulatives can be very helpful in teaching math concepts. For example, using blocks or counting bears to teach counting and basic addition and subtraction.

ii.   **Break tasks down into smaller steps:** Children with Down syndrome may have difficulty understanding complex instructions, so it's important to break tasks down into small, manageable steps. For example, when teaching reading, start with simple words and gradually build up to more complex words and sentences.

iii.   **Use hands-on activities:** Children with Down syndrome often learn best through hands-on activities, so incorporating these into math and reading lessons can be very beneficial. For example, use play dough to form letters of the alphabet or use a ruler to teach measurement concepts.

iv.   **Use positive reinforcement:** Children with Down syndrome may need extra encouragement and positive reinforcement to stay motivated.

A reward system such as a sticker chart can be a good way to keep a child engaged and motivated to learn.

v.   **Use technology**: There are many educational apps and games that can be used to teach math and reading to children with Down syndrome. For example, an app that uses pictures and audio to help teach letter and word recognition.

vi.   **Work with a team:** Children with Down syndrome often benefit from working with a team of specialists, including teachers, speech therapists, and occupational therapists. By working together, the team can develop a comprehensive approach to teaching math and reading that addresses the child's unique needs and strengths.

It's important to keep in mind that every child with Down syndrome is unique and may have different learning strengths and needs. These strategies may not work for every child, but with a little patience and creativity, it's possible to help a child with Down syndrome succeed in learning math and reading.

D. Encouraging social interactions and friendships

Start by including the child in social activities that are appropriate for their age and ability level. This could include play dates, sports teams, or youth groups.

Encourage participation in group activities where they can interact with their peers. This could include joining a community sports team, taking a class at a community center, or participating in a youth group.

Encourage the child to initiate interactions with others. This could include asking a friend to play or starting a conversation with a classmate.

Support the child in developing their communication skills. This could include speech therapy, social skills training, or other interventions.

Create opportunities for the child to spend time with their peers outside of structured activities. This could include inviting friends over for a play date or encouraging the child to invite a friend over to their house.

Lastly, be positive and patient, building friendships take time and effort, and for children with Down Syndrome, it may take a bit longer

E. Strategies for Teaching Social Skills and Self-Care

Teaching social skills and self-care to a child with Down syndrome can be challenging, but there are several strategies that can be used to make the process more effective. Here are some examples:

i. **Modeling:** Children with Down syndrome often learn best through modeling, so it's important to demonstrate the desired behavior. For example, if you want to teach the child how to shake hands, demonstrate the behavior and have the child practice with you.

ii. **Visual aids:** Children with Down syndrome may have difficulty processing verbal information, so visual aids such as pictures, diagrams, and videos can be very helpful in teaching social skills and self-care. For example, using a picture book or social story to teach appropriate social behaviors or using a visual schedule to teach self-care routines.

iii. **Role-playing:** Role-playing can be a fun and effective way to teach social skills and self-care. For example, have the child practice making introductions, taking turns in conversation, or asking for help in a role-playing scenario.

iv. **Repetition:** Children with Down syndrome may need extra practice to master new skills, so repetition is important. For example, practicing self-care routines such as brushing teeth or washing hands every day.

v. **Positive reinforcement**: Children with Down syndrome may need extra encouragement and positive reinforcement to stay motivated. A reward system such as a sticker chart can be a good way to keep a child engaged and motivated to learn.

vi. **Use technology:** There are many educational apps and games that can be used to teach social skills and self-care to children with Down syndrome. For example, an app that uses pictures and audio to help teach self-care routines or an app that uses interactive scenarios to teach appropriate social behaviors.

vii. **Work with a team:** Children with Down syndrome often benefit from working with a team of specialists, including teachers, speech therapists, and occupational therapists. By working together, the team can develop a comprehensive approach to teaching social skills and self-care that addresses the child's unique needs and strengths.

It's important to keep in mind that every child with Down syndrome is unique and may have different learning strengths and needs.

These strategies may not work for every child, but with a little patience and creativity, it's possible to help a child with Down syndrome succeed in learning social skills and self-care.

F. Teaching social skills and empathy

Teaching social skills and empathy to a child with Down Syndrome in a school setting is an important part of their overall development and inclusion in the classroom and community. Here are a few strategies that educators can use:

i.   **Model appropriate social behavior and interactions:** Children with Down syndrome often benefit from observing and mimicking the social behaviors of their peers and adults. By modeling appropriate social behavior, educators can help the child learn and practice new social skills.

ii. **Use role-playing and social stories:** Role-playing and social stories are effective tools for teaching social skills and empathy. They provide a safe and structured way for children to practice and understand different social situations and emotions.

iii. **Incorporate social skills instruction into daily activities:** Social skills and empathy can be taught in a variety of ways, including through activities such as cooperative games, group discussions, and class meetings.

iv. **Use social skills curriculum:** Specialized social skills curriculums can provide structured, step-by-step instruction on a wide range of social skills, including making friends, joining groups, and understanding emotions.

v. **Encourage participation in group activities:** Participating in group activities such as sports teams, music ensembles, and clubs can help children with Down syndrome learn and practice social skills in a natural and fun setting.

vi.   **Collaborate with specialists:** Collaborate with specialists such as speech therapists, occupational therapists and other professionals who can provide additional support in developing social skills and empathy.

It's important to remember that teaching social skills and empathy to a child with Down syndrome will require patience, and it may take longer for them to learn and internalize these skills. But with consistent and positive reinforcement, the child will be able to develop and improve on their social skills and empathy over time.

CHAPTER FOUR

CARING FOR A DOWN SYNDROME CHILD

Caring for a child with Down syndrome in school can involve a variety of strategies to help the child succeed academically and socially. Here are some examples of ways to care for a child with Down syndrome in school:

Individualized education plan (IEP): Each child with Down syndrome should have an individualized education plan (IEP) that outlines their specific needs and goals. The IEP should be reviewed and updated regularly in collaboration with teachers, parents, and specialists.

Adapting curriculum: Curriculum should be adapted to the child's abilities. For example, providing visual aids or breaking down tasks into smaller steps to help the child understand and complete assignments.

Inclusive education: Children with Down syndrome should be included in regular education classes as much as possible. This will give them the opportunity to interact with their peers and learn the same material as their classmates.

Positive reinforcement: Children with Down syndrome may need extra encouragement and positive reinforcement to stay motivated. A reward system such as a sticker chart can be a good way to keep a child engaged and motivated to learn.

Building self-esteem: Children with Down syndrome may have low self-esteem due to their learning challenges. Care should be taken to build the child's self-esteem by praising their efforts and accomplishments.

Social skills training: Children with Down syndrome may have difficulty with social interactions. Social skills training can help the child learn how to interact with their peers and develop friendships.

Collaboration: Collaboration between parents, caregivers, and teachers is crucial in providing effective care for a child with Down syndrome. Regular meetings can be held to discuss the child's progress and make adjustments as needed.

Access to specialists: Children with Down syndrome may require the services of specialists such as speech therapists, occupational therapists, and psychologists. Care should be taken to ensure that the child has access to these specialists as needed.

It's important to keep in mind that every child with Down syndrome is unique and may have different learning strengths and needs. Care for a child with Down syndrome in school should be tailored to the child's individual needs and goals. Collaboration and open communication between parents, caregivers, and teachers are crucial in providing effective care for a child with Down syndrome.

A. Health and Medical Considerations

Down syndrome is a genetic disorder caused by the presence of an extra copy of chromosome 21. It is characterized by physical and intellectual developmental delays. Children with Down syndrome may have certain health and medical considerations that need to be taken into account in the school setting.

i. **Developmental Delays**: Children with Down syndrome often have developmental delays, particularly in the areas of cognitive, speech, and language development. This means that they may need extra support in the classroom, such as special education services or extra help with reading and writing.

ii. **Physical Delays:** Children with Down syndrome may also have physical delays, such as low muscle tone and poor coordination. This can make it difficult for them to keep up with their peers in physical activities, such as running and playing sports. Physical therapy may be necessary to help them develop their motor skills.

iii.   **Cardiac Issues:** Children with Down syndrome have a higher risk of developing heart defects. These defects may require surgery or other treatments.

iv.   **Vision and Hearing Issues:** Children with Down syndrome may have vision and hearing problems, and may require regular check-ups with an ophthalmologist or audiologist.

v.   **Behavioral Issues:** Children with Down syndrome may have behavioral issues such as attention deficit disorder (ADD) or attention deficit hyperactivity disorder (ADHD). These behavioral issues may require therapy or medication.

B. Nutrition and Physical Activity

Nutrition and physical activity are important factors in the health and development of children with Down syndrome. Here are some specific ways that schools can support the nutrition and physical activity of a child with Down syndrome:

1. **Nutrition**: Schools can support the nutrition of a child with Down syndrome by providing healthy and appropriate meal options. This can include offering a variety of fruits and vegetables, lean proteins, and whole grains, as well as accommodating a variety of textures and flavors to encourage exploration of new foods. Schools can also work with the child's parents or caregivers to accommodate any dietary restrictions or allergies.

2. **Physical activity:** Schools can support the physical activity of a child with Down syndrome by providing opportunities for them to engage in regular physical activity. This can include recess, physical education classes, and structured activities

such as swimming, dance, or martial arts. Schools can also work with the child's parents or caregivers to identify any physical limitations or accommodations that may be needed.

3. **Adaptive equipment:** Schools can provide adaptive equipment such as adapted bicycles, tricycles, or swings, which can help children with Down syndrome to participate in physical activities and promote their motor development.

4. **Physical therapy:** Schools can work with physical therapists to develop a program that is appropriate for the child's physical abilities. This can include exercises to improve balance, coordination, and strength, as well as stretching and range-of-motion activities.

5. **Specialized programs:** Some schools may have specialized programs for children with Down syndrome that focus on physical activity and nutrition.

For example, this may include a dance or a swimming class where the child can learn new skills and have fun while getting physical activity.

It's important to note that every child is unique and may have different needs and abilities, so it is important to work with the child's parents or caregivers, as well as healthcare professionals to develop an individualized plan that will best support their health and development.

C. Emotional and Behavioral Support

Emotional and behavioral support is an important aspect of supporting a child with Down syndrome in school. Here are some specific ways that schools can provide emotional and behavioral support for a child with Down syndrome:

i. **Positive reinforcement**: Schools can use positive reinforcement techniques to encourage appropriate behavior and discourage negative behavior. This can include praising the child for good behavior, providing rewards for positive behavior, and redirecting the child's attention when they engage in negative behavior.

ii. **Social skills training**: Children with Down syndrome may need extra support in developing social skills. Schools can provide social skills training to help the child learn how to interact with peers, communicate effectively, and understand social cues.

iii. **Behavioral intervention**: Schools can work with a behavior specialist to develop a behavior intervention plan that addresses specific behaviors that the child may be struggling with. This may include strategies such as time-out, visual cues, and positive reinforcement.

iv. **Consistency**: Schools can provide consistency in the child's daily routine and expectations. This can include having a consistent schedule, using similar language and instructions, and providing a predictable and safe environment.

v. **Emotional support:** Children with Down syndrome may need extra emotional support to navigate the social and emotional demands of school. Schools can provide emotional support by having a counselor available to talk with the child, providing a safe space for the child to express their emotions, and working with the child's parents or caregivers to address any emotional or behavioral concerns.

vi.   Inclusive approach: Schools can take an inclusive approach to education by including children with Down syndrome in regular classes and activities. This can include providing accommodations such as extra time for assignments or visual aids, and providing support to the child's classmates to help them understand and accept their peers with Down syndrome.

It's important to note that every child is unique and may have different emotional and behavioral needs and abilities, so it is important to work with the child's parents or caregivers, as well as healthcare professionals to develop an individualized plan that will best support their emotional and behavioral well-being.

D. Building Resilience and Self-Esteem

Building resilience and self-esteem in children with Down syndrome is an important aspect of their development and education. Here are a few strategies that can be used to support these children in school:

Encourage positive self-talk: Children with Down syndrome may struggle with self-doubt and negative self-talk. Encourage them to speak positively about themselves and their abilities. For example, "I am smart" or "I can do it."

Provide opportunities for success: Set up situations where the child can succeed and feel a sense of accomplishment. For example, assigning tasks that are challenging but not too difficult, or giving them responsibilities within the classroom that are within their abilities.

Celebrate small successes: Recognize and celebrate small successes and improvements.

For example, if a child has difficulty with fine motor skills, acknowledge when they have improved their penmanship.

Teach coping strategies: Children with Down syndrome may have a harder time dealing with stress and difficult situations. Teaching them coping strategies such as deep breathing, visualization, or positive self-talk can help them manage their emotions.

Encourage independence: Encourage children with Down syndrome to be independent and make their own choices. For example, allowing them to choose their own clothes or snacks can help them build self-esteem and self-confidence.

Provide a positive and supportive environment: Create a positive and supportive classroom environment where children feel safe to take risks and make mistakes. Example:

A teacher can provide opportunities for success by giving a child with Down syndrome the task of putting away the classroom library books. The teacher can recognize and celebrate the child's success by praising them for their hard work and keeping track of their progress. Additionally, the teacher can teach coping strategies by encouraging the child to take deep breaths when they feel overwhelmed and remind them to speak positively to themselves. This can help the child manage their emotions and build resilience.

It is important to remember that every child with Down syndrome is unique and may have different needs and abilities. It is essential to work closely with parents, caregivers, and other professionals to develop an individualized plan that supports the child's strengths and addresses their needs.

CONCLUSION

Managing and caring for a child with Down syndrome in school requires a holistic approach that addresses the child's individual needs and abilities. It is essential to work closely with parents, caregivers, and other professionals to develop an individualized plan that supports the child's strengths and addresses their needs.

One of the most important things to keep in mind when working with a child with Down syndrome is to provide a positive and supportive environment. This includes setting up situations where the child can succeed and feel a sense of accomplishment, recognizing and celebrating small successes, and creating a classroom culture that is inclusive and accepting.

Another key aspect of managing and caring for a child with Down syndrome in school is teaching coping strategies and encouraging independence. Teaching children how to manage their emotions, how to take deep breaths, how to visualize, and how to speak positively to themselves and can help them manage stress and difficult situations.

Encouraging independence by allowing children to make their own choices can also help them build self-esteem and self-confidence.

It is also important to remember that children with Down syndrome may have different needs and abilities than their peers. For example, they may have difficulty with fine motor skills, have short attention span, or have difficulty with abstract concepts. It is essential to be patient and understanding of these challenges, and to provide support and accommodations to help the child succeed.

In conclusion, managing and caring for a child with Down syndrome in school requires a holistic approach that addresses the child's individual needs and abilities. It is essential to work closely with parents, caregivers, and other professionals to develop an individualized plan that supports the child's strengths and addresses their needs. Providing a positive and supportive environment, teaching coping strategies, and encouraging independence are key strategies for helping children with Down syndrome succeed in school

Summary of Key Points

- Provide clear and consistent structure and routines in the classroom.

- Use visual aids and other forms of alternative communication to supplement verbal instruction.

- Break down tasks into smaller, manageable steps.

- Use positive reinforcement and rewards to encourage appropriate behavior.

- Provide opportunities for physical activity and movement to help with attention and focus.

- Collaborate with parents and other specialists, such as speech therapists and occupational therapists, to ensure a comprehensive approach to the child's education.

- Differentiate instruction to meet the child's individual needs and abilities.

- Foster a positive and inclusive classroom environment that values and celebrates the child's unique strengths and contributions

Additional Resources for Families and Educators

- National Down Syndrome Society (NDSS) - This organization provides resources and support for families and educators of children with Down Syndrome, including information on education and advocacy.

- Down Syndrome Education International - This organization provides information and resources on evidence-based education for children with Down Syndrome, including training and support for educators.

- "Inclusive Education for Students with Down Syndrome: A Guide for Teachers" by Dr. Thomas E. Pomeranz - This book provides a comprehensive guide for educators on how to support students with Down Syndrome in inclusive classrooms.

- "The Down Syndrome Educational Trust" - The DSE is a UK based charity which provides information, support and training for parents, carers and professionals working with people with Down syndrome.

- "Down Syndrome Association of America" - DSA provides a wide range of resources and support for families and educators of children with Down Syndrome, including information on education, advocacy, and community events.

- The National Center for Special Education Research (NCSER) - This center conducts and supports research to improve educational outcomes for children with disabilities, including those with Down Syndrome.

- "Supporting Students with Down Syndrome: A Guide for Teachers" by Dr. Maryanne Wolf - This book provides practical strategies and resources for educators to support the learning and development of students with Down Syndrome.

It is important to note that each child with Down Syndrome is unique and may require different approaches and strategies in the classroom, so it is important to work closely with the child's parents and specialists to determine the best approach for the individual child.

Recap of key strategies for raising a happy child with Down syndrome

- Provide clear and consistent structure and routines in the home and daily life.
- Use visual aids and other forms of alternative communication to supplement verbal instruction.
- Encourage and support the child's interests and strengths.
- Use positive reinforcement and rewards to encourage appropriate behavior.
- Provide opportunities for physical activity and movement.
- Foster a positive and inclusive environment that values and celebrates the child's unique strengths and contributions.
- Develop a strong partnership with the child's parents, specialists, and educators to ensure a comprehensive approach to the child's development.

- Encourage independence and self-care skills as the child grows older.

- Provide regular social interactions, friendships and inclusive activities for the child to participate in.

- Be patient, understanding, and kind as the child may learn at a slower pace than others. Remember to celebrate small achievements as well as bigger ones.

Made in United States
Orlando, FL
02 October 2024

52242045R00039